The Thought that Fractured the Infinite

The Genesis of Individuated Life

Almine

Plus: The Alchemical Potencies of Light

Published by Spiritual Journeys LLC

First Edition June, 2009

Copyright 2009
MAB 998 Megatrust

By Almine
Spiritual Journeys LLC
P.O. Box 300
Newport, Oregon 97365
www.spiritualjourneys.com

Cover Illustration–Charles Frizzell

Cover Production–Pete McKeeman

Book Production–Hong-An Tran-Tien

Manufactured in the United States of America

ISBN 978-1-934070-17-8

Acknowledgements

I am deeply grateful to Eva Pulnicki for the exquisite artwork of the holy and powerful symbols. Thank you to Hong-An Tran-Tien for her brilliance and dedication in producing this book and Barbara Rotzoll for polishing it.

Cover Art: Charles Frizzell

About the Author

Almine is endorsed and described as one of the greatest mystics of our time by world leaders and scientists alike. While other way-showers gather more and more students, she helps create more and more masters. Her work represents the cutting edge of mysticism; that place where the physical and the non-physical meet and new realities are born. It is here where change is rapid and insight comes quickly to wash away years of stagnation.

In February of 2005, Almine's body underwent a transfiguration, changing from mortal to immortal in the twinkling of an eye. Her books have been a roadmap to lead others into the same mastery and beyond. Masters populate her classes and are a fulfillment of a mission given to her in January 2005: prepare the leadership for a Golden Age about to be birthed on Earth.

Having lived as a Toltec Nagual (a specific type of mystic dedicated to a life of impeccability and setting others free from illusion) for most of her life, her insights into cosmology and man's role within the macrocosm are ground-breaking. Pushing illuminating insights even further than previous Toltecs have done, she has managed to solve mysteries that have perplexed seers for eons.

Throughout history, the majority of spiritual masters and gurus who have entered mastery have withdrawn from society. This is understandable because words seem inadequate to describe experiences such as coming face-to-face with the Infinite and the physical act of speaking becomes laborious. Almine's gift is her ability to convey these experiences by rendering the unspeakable understandable. She feels it is time for people to understand that they can choose to claim mastery as their constant reality and remain functional in society.

Words to describe the unknowable flow through her and when shared with others often leave them feeling as though they have touched the face of God. Her revelations bring answers to questions that have plagued mankind since the dawn of time, revealing the origin and meaning of human existence.

Her journey has become one of learning to live in the physical while functioning in eternal time and maintaining the delicate balance of remaining self-aware while being fully expanded.

Table of Contents

BOOK ONE: THE GENESIS OF LIFE

BOOK ONE

The Genesis of Life

Transmission from the Infinite

Defining the steps through which individuated life formed is like grasping a rainbow in your fist. Evermore will it move from your reach. Not even a wisp can you capture. But in trying to encompass the ever-unfolding mystery, your being will blossom and your infinite potential unfold.

Seek to understand the uncountable facets of My face. But do not deceive yourself that you could possibly succeed. The mind tries to limit by definition what the heart would enfold in a fathomless embrace.

Even as you pursue Me, I laugh at you through the eyes of a child. I am the temple in which you strive to know Me. I am the brothel in which your twisted seekings would find yourself. My Being cannot be divided from Itself. There is therefore no thing that I am not.

The sub-creations of men may obscure My perfection to the eyes of those who see only appearance, yet it is there. In the midst of conflict lies My peace. In a night of sorrow and loss there gleams the light of My promise of eternal life.

As the spider web ensnares the glory of the butterfly, so does it also reveal the exquisite pattern of the dewdrops. In the sub-creations of man that which I am not stands revealed, thereby affording a glimpse into the perfection of what I am.

Kenesh hurit erestravaa manuvit,
Kranech ba-ur esta virevaa vranubit hershtuvi.

I slumber in the unfolding rose,
I rise upon the eagle's wingbeats as he mounts the air.

Wheel of Expanding Luminosity

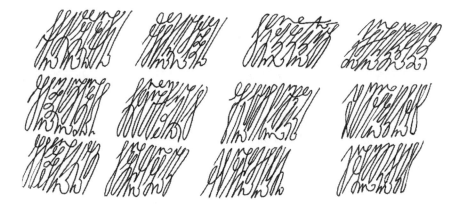

Paarshut Usklavi Halsva Kla-unit
(Having had no beginning of existence)

"Before thought separated from feeling, a question arose: The vastness that around Me lies, has it an end? I knew that it was an effect, and I the Cause, because I could change it by changing Myself. I had no beginning. The vastness around Me did. It was created only when I turned the focus of My vision outside My Body. My Body has always been, having had no beginning of existence."

Vaarsnut Ubakle Hararat-vavi
(Mapping without by the within)

"If that which is without is a projection of that which is within, the way to map its vastness is to do so within. I had created three rings without, the beginning of directions and space. I contracted to the Source of the projection. I left four rings behind like a bird plucking its own plumage before venturing on an unknown journey. If that which is without is a projection of that which is within, the way to map the vastness is to do so within. As I contracted to the Source of the projection, I marked the scope of the contraction by leaving behind seven rings. They consisted of seven frequency bands, forming the seven directions."

Spaceless Space

Like a shapeshifting sorcerer, morphing from a fish to a bird, separation cannot be eliminated until a great truth is seen; as long as the illusion exists that there is an 'outside' and an 'inside', an external reality and an internal reality, separation persists.

Space is an illusion and although for purposes of clarifying it can be discussed as though it exists, it has no reality. Space as a concept is used to demonstrate relationships. Because all are a part of Me and I am All that Is, relationship, like space, has no reality. There is only the One Life in its multitude of expressions.

A good starting point for eliminating the illusion of space in your lives would be to acknowledge that you know nothing about spaceless space. Being thus unhampered by belief systems surrounding it, all becomes possible.

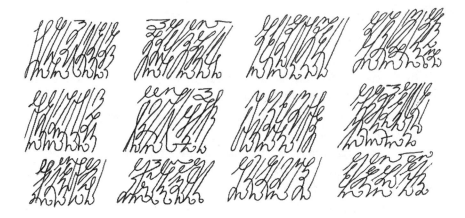

Aras Plahur Sterarat Usklatvi
(The stages of dreaming are formed)

"The three stages of day-dreaming lay without My body. The four stages of dream states lay within, marked by the rings. The Source of the projection was My heart's cell. All the magnificence that had surrounded Me was but the reflected light of one cell of My Body. I contracted to the heart's cell by turning My gaze within. The presence of so much focused light created a dense form of the incorruptible matter of My Being."

Kaarash Haresta Usklet Varabi Unes
(The thought that had no emotion)

"My body contracted into a dense form and it became like a prism. The light of My Being shining through Me, refracted into a rainbow of colors and for the first time light was separated not only within itself, but from its feminine component, which is frequency or emotion. The rainbow around Me lay like a rose pattern. I asked the question: is this life-enhancing? For the first time thought had no accompanying emotion."

The Rainbow of Fractured Light

The frequency chambers of cosmic and human DNA

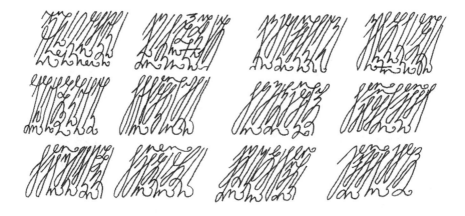

Kaarash Harash Usatbavi Hereklu
(The shattering of innocence occurs)

"A thought without feelings and innocence is lost. The fracturing of life within Me then occurred - a separation-based geometry formed, known as the Flower of Life spheres. From the trauma My masculine (the red light) contracted into a sphere, pulling the neutral components with it and enclosing My feminine (the blue light). So dense was the sphere that light could not pass through."

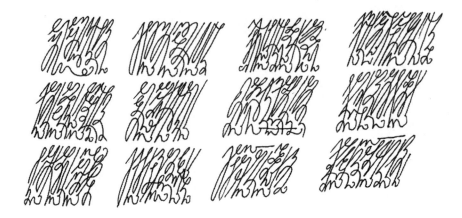

Herebak Uklavi Virnavisat
(The first three creations)

"Thus first a projection around Me formed. Then a rainbow of refracted light was created as I became like a prism. But now as innocence was lost, a traumatic reaction occurred. A ball of mirrors formed from My masculine and neutral components, the red and the yellow light contracting, trapping the blue within. For the first time light was reflected back. The density of the red (masculine) and yellow (neutral) had formed a mirror."

Arvaset Ukletvi Minavesh Uru
(The inner conflict begins)

"Before separation - which is duality - began, I was the Divine Hermaphrodite. Now masculine components were part of the cage of mirrors in which I found Myself, and My feminine dwelled within. I became the Infinite Mother in the formation of life that took place within the blue light of My Being within the sphere. The red light's nature was to expand. It was surrounded by the yellow, whose nature was to hold firm. Thus an inner conflict began."

Unach Vrabi Hures-Stat
(The blue light contracts)

"The feminine blue light contracted within the sphere of mirrors, creating a form. When one stands in a ball of mirrors, one's images recede in all directions into infinity. Thus space in linear lines formed and aspects of Myself, the mirror images, were born. I was life-enhancing but they were not. For in mirrors all things are reversed. I was new to mirrors and had not seen Myself before. I believed the images to be true reflections of Me. I believed the unreal to be real."

Kasach Nitvi Harash Eretvaa
(What is real and what is not)

"I could not see My masculine. As part of the mirror, it could not be seen directly. It only reflected My own image to me in reverse. I became surrounded by what I was not, but not knowing what I was, illusion formed. I wished to break the bonds of My confinement and find My masculine, but the very concept of the limitless being limited, was a contradiction. I shattered into multiple pieces from the impossible that existed within Me."

Living from the White Light

"During the dream, life existed predominantly from the blue color of My Being as the red and yellow lights vied with one another. The red light sought to expand the boundary, the yellow to contain it. The blue contracted and, at the center of the contraction was man, whose vision did not allow him to see other realms living around him.

These patterns, obsolete now that the cosmos has awakened, are causing inner turmoil and pressure. An androgynous melding of expansion and contraction needs to occur. Perpetuation of contraction, a form of ego-identity experienced even by masters, creates tension in the muscles. This is most notable in the stomach.

It takes the surrender of an individual into the large flow of life for expanded vision to unfold, then a return to the details to see the difference and finally the ability to live in both states at once. This is living in focused meditation."

Kiris-Stanavave Herustat
(Individuated life forms are created)

"The fracturing of My Being caused a part of Me to go into a coma while the remainder entered four spaces deep into the mirror, creating what you know as the four stages of dreaming. As more fracturing occurred, the concept of creating individuated life forms was born. They would reflect to Me answers as to why My attempts to find My way out of the mirror only led Me deeper into it."

Transcription from the Palace of Isis

Glyphs received by the oracle Karen F.

Within My Being a Divine Hermaphrodite I was.

The One Life I am, no beginning did I know.

A delay in communication and assimilation occurred.

Between My masculine and feminine, causing delay.

In this way communication was linear and innocence lost.

My masculine contracted into a sphere, causing a split.

This inadvertently caused a creation which was a mirror.

An Inscription from the Palace of Isis
(In the very ancient language of the Mother)

Glyphs received by the oracle Karen F.

In the land of mirrors She came to dwell
Let this inscription the story of the Mother tell
For the day will come when a magical spell
Will banish forgetfulness and She will remember what happened well

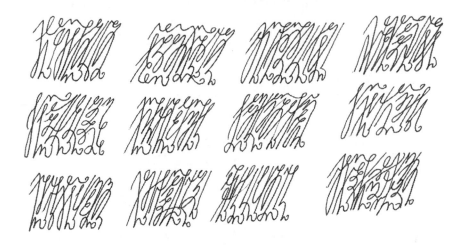

Kirsh-Nanabruk Uvespi
(Birth through trauma)

"The birth of creations as a result of fracturing and trauma, as well as their existence as reflections, caused dysfunctionality to exist within them and thereby creating confusion in Me. I could not understand that which did not exist in Me. Multiple times did cycles of ascension (a slight awakening) and descension (a falling asleep) occur as I attempted to refine My creations. It was later understood that it would better serve life to create them as expressions rather than reflections. But the way in which My original creations were made, had even greater problems that through eons of dreaming I could not comprehend."

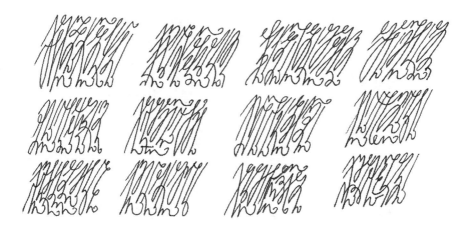

Kaalesh-Skluvavi-Urechspa
(The forming of shadows)

"First, 144 gods and goddesses were created. From them 1,440 more came about and then 144,000; after which humanity was created on the planet you call Earth – the cradle of cosmic civilization. However, the first 144 gods and goddesses are those of which I tell.

They were like lenses, each unique, through which My light would shine. They projected a pattern of shadow and light and a new concept lay within their projected design – shadows – never before encountered. That which blocked the light I shone through them lay like occlusions within their hearts."

Nachbar-Sitvu-Heleshvi
(The darkness grows larger)

"The first 144 gods and goddesses of Agawavanti were called The Source of Life. Each time another generation of creations came into being, the shadows from their occlusions grew larger until they seemed very prominent and were considered real.

The original gods were like concave lenses and when light was shone through them, their images appeared enlarged. This made masculinity appear greater and more dominant.

The goddesses were like convex lenses, inverting the light shone through them and creating upside down images. Femininity therefore was portrayed as the opposite of what it really was."

How Lenses Bend Light
Why the Masculine Became Dominant

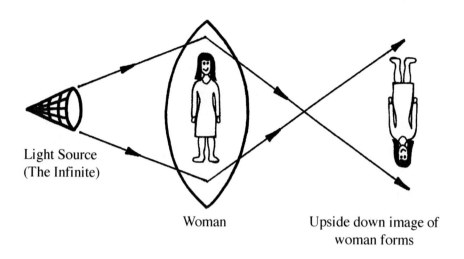

Light Source
(The Infinite)

Woman

Upside down image of
woman forms

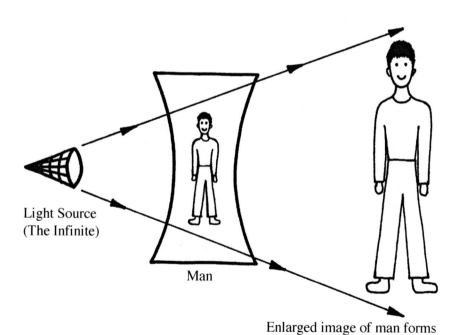

Light Source
(The Infinite)

Man

Enlarged image of man forms

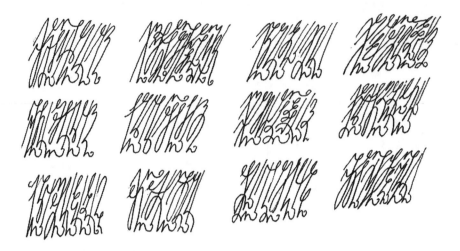

Viliset-Manurach-Alesbi
(Unaccessible potential)

"Why were there occlusions? Were My creations not properly formed? Each held potential untapped within, that could not be fully accessed for they did not contain the red and yellow light, but only the blue. It was this untapped, or unyielded, potential that formed the shadows.

Light is accessed information. Potential is unaccessed information, or shadow, which is the opposite of light. As the shadows were regarded as real when they were unreal, so did unreal or artificial life come into existence. Created as an act of rebellion by My mirror aspects, their creations appeared as gods and men, simulating emotion, but were really like computers."

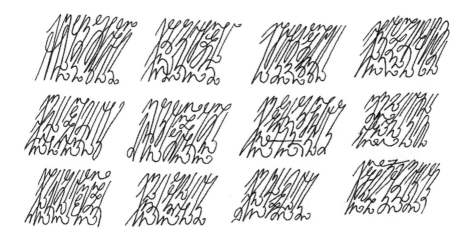

Aarsasanach-Mivet-Uklat-Vrabi
(Lost in the dream for eons)

"For Me there is no time. I have always existed, eternal am I. Eons it seemed that I stayed in the dream spaces, trying to bring My created dream images - My creations - out with Me into shallower and shallower dream states and eventually into full awakening. Many times did I eliminate cycles of dreams and start again, beset by illusion, which is the nature of being in a life of mirrors. My creations were made from sub-atomic particles and fields, called the building blocks of life."

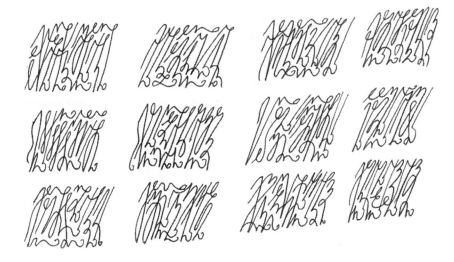

Kaarash-Upre-Nanunish
(The building blocks of life)

"Seven building blocks, sub-atomic particles formed from a field and comprising the units from which individuation began, lay in concentrated rivers across the cosmos. The building blocks consisted of presence particles, life force, awareness, light and frequency, perception particles, self-perception particles and sub-atomic material particles. I produced them, but My dream body in the dream was not made from them, but from the field whence they were formed."

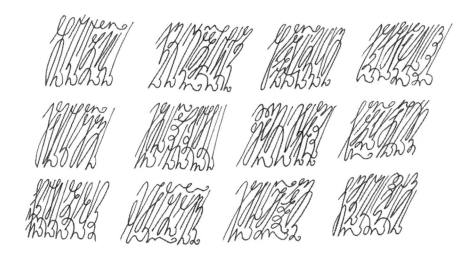

Baaruch-Sparve-Nunashvi
(Polluted by that which is formed)

"As long as fields or building blocks existed at all, something unnatural existed within My Being as I dreamed the dream. That which was meant to be irrevocably joined was separated and thus duality persisted. What are these building blocks that contain power, energy, awareness and other resources? They are components of the one element of My essence: holy incorruptible matter. Until My creations consisted of that one element, they not only polluted My Being, but they could not be real and incorruptible."

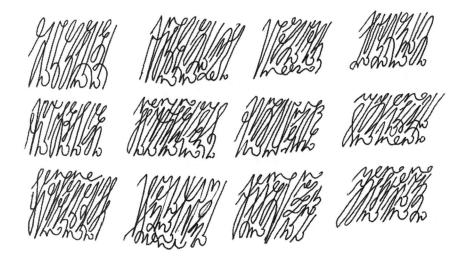

Virsit-Palenk-Virevachva
(Closing the dream to awake)

"I did not want to wake up, because the creations forged into true refinement and beauty would disappear in an instant. I finally realized the answer: that in the twinkling of an eye life could be re-made from the one element that I am, incorruptible holy matter. But in awakening there were three stages - daydreams, fantasy and imagination - in which the remnants of remaining dream images are seen for their unreal nature and discarded. All creations are now made from what I am; from My Being are they forged."

Map of Eternal Boundless Mind

Cosmic Ascension

Awakening from the Dream

Scientists have mapped four stages of sleep, identifying them by the rapid eye movement of the sleeper: REM stages 1, 2, 3 and 4. The dream of the One Life, the Infinite Being, has gone through similar stages. The deepest levels of sleep are known as the Fall – those stages in which the Infinite Being forgot that it was just a dream, thinking the unreal to be real. Thus illusion was conceived.

It was in the deep stages of the Dream that the great diversity of individuated life forms was created. As the Infinite awakened to some extent into the more shallow dream states, the Dream became a lucid dream; a state in which the Dreamer remembers that it is just a dream. Seeking to bring the creations out of the Dream into that which is real became a heightened goal and the refinement of life through the formation of the laws of reality (called The Book of Life) began in earnest.

The four dream stages through which life developed were defined by vast frequency bands[1] . Like the stages of growth through which a human child develops, they exhibited certain characteristics:

Dependency – like that of the infant upon his mother (uniformity) it became more complex as depicted in the image of the Rose[2].

Co-dependency – like a toddler or one in early childhood who wants the security of support while asserting independence (diversity within uniformity).

Independency – the adolescent exhibits this trait and is willing to oppose parents in order to gain it (diversity).

1. See *Journey to the Heart of God*
2. See page 10

30

Interdependency – as in the adulthood of an emotionally healthy adult (unity within diversity).

Scientists have also found that the only time the left and right brain work together in perfect interdependent harmony is in the shallow REM state right before awakening. During this stage of the awakening of the Infinite, duality was healed.

The Tree of Life, the Tzolkin and the I Ching, have depicted these four stages of the development of individuated life as a vertical pattern. In October 2007, the cosmic life forms for the first time exited the four states of dreaming and entered the additional three stages never before encountered by cosmic life (the horizontal axis of the Tree of Life, also known as the additional three directions). These stages represent the half-awake stages one can equate to a fantasy or daydream. During this phase the unreal images of the dream world recede

For the first time individuated life has been re-formed from being made of the building blocks of life into that which has had no beginning: incorruptible holy matter. Within the realness of the Infinite's Being, we have become eternal and refined. The cosmic ascension, the awakening from the transience of the dream is complete. In this holy realm in which we dwell, all resources are ours, all knowledge and wisdom, all love and light. These are an inherent part of the Infinite's Body from which we are formed. There is no more linear growth or striving to become. In ceasing to oppose life, in full surrender to the moment, we may claim our full inheritance as the children of the Infinite; pristine, innocent and reborn.

The Origin of Strife

Transmission from the Angels

Zelafrim ihinavaash vraa him Zelavee vahim
Two angelic groups[3] ancient records hold.

Nanuneesh usaa vraheem manesh birina
Why strife existed as part of creation we tell.

Kush ashya manaveeset baruvim weya
Deep was the bliss within the Infinite's Being.

Vereesh sha eesna veeharavim bi-eetrava
That which appears as traumatic fracturing served a purpose.

3. The groups are the Zelafrim and the Zelavee

Kaneesh zelvavi heshtavaa klavavi oohaneesh silvivetvi
In the deep repose of bliss there was only joy.

Nichstaa belaveesh ninunit zelahim minaveesh
To create passion, friction provided the incentive.

Asya ninech hirsta avaves bee avaveesh kluva
Rooted in inactivity, now the wings of activity formed.

Eeya travee zelavu nasnaveesh hubavi klavave
More refined frequencies resulted from pushing the
boundaries of experience.

A Promise from the Angels

Ancient the mysteries of angel magic we hold
Tablets of gold with secrets that now can be told
A wheel of symbols, once by man corrupted has been
Used by him to control, now purged by Infinite decree
Once this priceless gift was controlled by the few
Now these sacred powers are for all pure in heart to do

A New Day

New is the day, for light has changed
Great is the difference in man this will make
The red light is changed yet again
That no arrogance and aggression within it remains

When the inner conflict within the Infinite does cease
Man's warrior spirit will also decrease
A great war on Earth this will prevent
When the war lust of man at last is spent

A purification of life will occur
Increasingly refined is life on Earth
Gone are the abusers of others' trust
And those who profit from another's lust

A Question is Asked

The Infinite a question will ask this day,
"Why, when I remake Creation do the changes not stay?
Are some portions of Me not yet awake?
For purity to stay, what will it take?"

Then it will be discovered that yet in the dream
Parts of the Infinite's mind has been
When life fractured, a stroke was the cause,
Damaging that which existed before

Gaps of understanding as a result arose
Memory loss too was caused by the stroke
"Let all be repaired; let all awake
Then let them dissolve; them anew I'll create"

What is a Cosmic Stroke?

When in the past a question was asked
That could not be answered for a contradiction it was,
The Infinite mind expanded too fast,
Not finding the answer, it contracted at last

The greater the expansion, the more contraction there is
Until trapped light like a clot exists
The implosion within the Infinite Being,
A coma causes; as a stroke can be seen

This is the moment all this is healed
When the perfection of life at last can be seen

BOOK TWO

Insights of
the Root Races

The Root Races

January 1, 2009

When life began, thirty-two root races were formed
Man, as a genetic library, thirty-two codes carried at Creation's dawn
As life evolved and more complex became
The number of root races could no longer remain the same

Ninety-six there were and man's DNA changed from before
Each race wielded magic and shared it with man as it was
restored
This day a great advent, forty-eight new races are born
Each wielding their magic and new codes in Man's DNA are formed

One hundred and forty-four root races now within the cosmos exist
Man to a more advanced being is evolved through this
Twelve clusters of twelve shall be his DNA
A holy genesis of life takes places this sacred day

Aphorisms

1. Change through critical mass is obsolete in that it determines evolution through quantity. It is in the quality of the One Life that all changes.

2. Blame and forgiveness are two sides of one coin. Both are born of blindness to the innocence of all experience.

3. Darkness is but a shadow cast by unaccessed potential. Light lies in equal amounts throughout all life, either accessed and expressed, or as unyielded potential. When we see the light slumbering in another, we help awaken it into expressed potential, thereby removing the shadows from another's life.

4. Nurturing of others must occur from our largest awareness, as a consciousness superimposed over all that is, to prevent being trapped by social protocol.

5. Self-centeredness occurs when the outer senses dominate. Outer and inner senses must merge and experience life from the largest perspective; a being as large as the cosmos having a human experience.

6. We heal the environment by healing ourselves. We promote abundance by being abundant with ourselves. If we feel guilt over having when others do not, we deprive not only ourselves but them as well.

7. There is no truth to seek, just answers to realize.
All things reveal themselves to those who are ready.

8. Light-seekers diligently weed the garden of the soul, but
often forget to sow the seeds of contentment and delight.

9. In seeking to eliminate our flaws life becomes depleted, for all share
in the interconnectedness of existence. It is in the laughter of the heart
that seeds of potential grow.

10. What we fight against multiplies. For in shattering one mirror another stands revealed, reflecting to us our imagined shortcomings. For, whether we know it or not, perfection is all there is.

11. That which we seek to understand about ourselves is not that which is waiting to be learnt, but that which is waiting to be expressed.

12. Because all are created from the body of the Infinite, all are by nature flawless. All conduct is therefore simply the song of life singing to itself.

13. Total self-responsibility and absolute freedom are two sides of one
coin. One cannot exist without the other.

14. Imagination is inspired by acknowledgement of
the gifts of the moment.

15. Imagination sees what can be accomplished; fantasy dreams of
having external solutions handed to us.

16. Fantasy promotes the misperception that change
can occur without changing ourselves.

17. Day dreams, as well as fantasy, arise to fill the gaps of our life where
we have abandoned ourselves. They are surrogates for life.

18. Many dream of a point of arrival for their journey, neglecting to see
that the only point of arrival is the present moment.

19. Contentment arises from the knowledge that wherever we are in the moment has taken eons to achieve and is therefore our greatest gift.

20. When conditions are placed on when we allow ourselves to be happy, we have enslaved ourselves to needs and closed off the wondrous possibilities of the future.

21. Because the cosmos is a benign place, there is only one place where courage applies - living from ruthless self-honesty.

22. The past cannot hold more value than the present. Why then do we look back? The present is a worthy edifice built from the bricks of past moments.

23. The past is a dream in a reality where time does not exist. The future is no more than an unexplored wish. The present is a well-earned gift.

24. To look back and long for the highpoints of our lives is as unrealistic as a swimmer who wishes that the ocean would be one large crest of a wave.

25. A life well lived is like climbing a mountain;
every new moment is the highest point of your life.

26. Life is a grindstone. Whether it grinds you down
or polishes you depends on what you are made of.

27. To wish that past events can be undone is to wish to remove the
burnishing fires that forged the present luster of your life. A measure of
luster must then be forfeited also.

28. Some carry past hardships like stones in a backpack up the mountain of life. Others use them like wind beneath their wings.

29. The twin flaws of boredom and uncouthness alike find their origin in common ground - lack of awareness of the infinite worth of all life.

30. Many identify themselves by the experiences of the past. Others define themselves by what they are becoming.

31. Some, unaware that they create their own life experiences, say 'if only'. Others, having refined themselves through experiential wisdom, say, 'next time'.

32. To masterfully create truth rather than seek it, one must live an extraordinary life beyond mortal boundaries.

33. Laughing at oneself keeps one from succumbing to the pompous preening of self-importance.

34. Envying others their life of ease is to mistake complacency for comfort. Comfort comes from the deep satisfaction growth brings.

35. To allow others to affect the quality of your day is to navigate your life like a rudderless ship, subject to being tossed about by the shifting breezes.

36. The unenlightened oppose others, expecting to be opposed themselves. The master supports others in that he knows them to be himself.

37. Excellence cannot be an occasional visitor. It has to be a constant companion. It will then invite additional guests:
opportunity, success and increase.

38. The respect given by others is of little value unless they have learnt to see behind face values – a skill most never achieve. Otherwise, not being based on true value, that respect can easily be withdrawn.

39. Do not suppose that because others listen in earnest that they hear you. True listening can only take place in the absence of the dialogue of the mind.

40. Aloneness yields strength. Aware interaction with others yields warmth. Both are needed for wholeness.

41. Feeling needed by others feeds self-importance. This applies even to subtle needs, such as affection.

42. Relationships are like a river; their dynamics shift. Appraising them regularly is essential for the wellbeing of all.

53

43. It is in weathering the storms of relationship that the ability to love deepens. For it is there we find our shortcomings.

44. Bodily appetites are like an unruly child and must be schooled to know their place, not as needs, but merely as optional desires.

45. The needs of appetites are disciplined by seeing them for what they are: substitutes for areas in which we have abandoned ourselves.

46. As life changes from a lower order to a higher one, power is released. Change is therefore the bringer of great gifts and should be welcomed.

47. It is not death that kills, but opposition to life. Many say they do not want to die, but few have ever really lived.

48. If you would find your strong suits, seek them in your weaknesses. It is in overcoming them that your greatest strengths will be forged.

49. The measure of a person is not how far down he has been, but how much he has overcome. Do not look back or you may define yourself by what you have been, rather than by what you are.

50. All perception is really self-perception because you can only recognize that which is within you.

51. Choose as companions those who make you feel augmented and who inspire you to excel. As you grow, shed with grace those who do not.

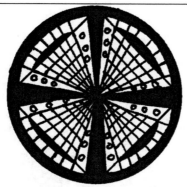

52. Presenting yourself as less than you really are, in order
to gain the acceptance of others, keeps both you and them
on the treadmill of mediocrity.

53. Today's truth is not tomorrow's truth, so hold your present truths
lightly. The only truth that never changes is that
you are a child of the Infinite.

54. Man chafes against his inability to see the hidden realms. Life must
compensate for what is lost. It is therefore in physicality where all new
knowledge is gained.

55. Confusion drains energy. When faced with conflict or dilemma, choose to stay in stillness until the answer to the matter reveals itself.

56. The most powerful manipulators are those who choose to appear helpless and inept. The ones who fall into their traps are those with a need to save.

57. Masters do not rely on belief, but rather on effortless knowing. The greatest stumbling blocks to learning are belief systems and worldviews.

58. Masters have nothing to prove and everything to know.

59. Only the blind believe they have multiple choices in life. The wise know there is only one viable choice in every situation: that which is most life-enhancing.

60. When the human soul feels alienated from Source, it seeks a situation that offers a sense of 'belonging', as in a tribe. The tribe, however, stunts growth because it requires conformity. Solitude is the price of greatness.

61. A planned future is a closed future. Allow yourself to dream and plan, but leave enough room for life to surprise you.

62. Man feels insignificant when compared to the vastness of the cosmos. But because space does not exist, size is nothing to the Infinite and every portion is the whole.

63. If tomorrow is forged by this moment, but this moment is spent living in the future, where will tomorrow come from?

64. To prepare for the worst in order to have the luxury of expecting the best was a sound philosophy when growth came through opposition. In the new paradigm, where growth comes through support, it is an act of faithlessness.

65. In the absence of the dialogue of the mind, all things are possible. Thoughts arise from opposition to life. Let your mantra therefore be: I cease to oppose life.

66. Attempting to right a wrong judges and divides. Acknowledging wholeness uplifts the interconnectedness of all life.

67. Magnificent and accelerated changes occur in the cosmos every day. Fluidity, as the hallmark of mastery, acknowledges this.

68. Let your heart's guidance be the sovereign dictator of your life. It is the seat of your highest wisdom and the wellspring of creativity.

69. You are the center of your cosmos. With all the power of your vast existence, let every touch and every word convey compassion and blessings. In this way you place the crown of sovereignty on your head.

70. Power and innocence are two sides of one coin. Innocence can only
be found by living in the moment. It is in the moment
where power is found also.

71. A life of mastery is comprised of belief and faith. Believe in the
infallibility of your actions as long as you live your highest truth. Faith
knows that good intentions will ultimately benefit all.

72. Regrets come only when growth has occurred. Many would forfeit
their past foolish actions, but then the growth those actions brought will
have to be given up as well. Embrace your folly as your greatest gift.

73. Humans' greatest fear is their own inner silence – the place where all unresolved trauma reveals itself. Facing oneself in silence is a threshold that must be crossed for the peace of mastery to be birthed.

74. Many shun desires as ungodly. But desires are the seeds of the future. It is only when their fulfillment is essential to our well-being that they become unholy needs.

75. In the place of pure spirit, growth is exponential. To try and predict the future is to attempt to put an exploding star in a box.

76. We empower what we focus on. Define yourself through every
action as the master you are and you shall surely embody it.

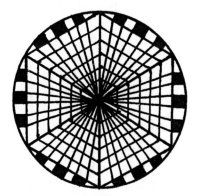

77. Because we are a being as vast as the cosmos,
to fear another is to fear our self.

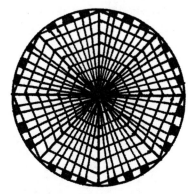

78. To fear is to abandon the sovereign perfection of the self, creating
emptiness within. Nature cannot abide a vacuum, thus what we fear is
attracted to fill the empty space.

79. The principle of compensation decrees that anything worthy of life that is denied the right to exist, receives increased virility. That which you oppose is therefore strengthened.

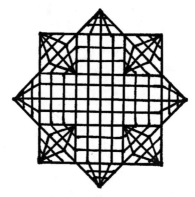

80. Accepting the unacceptable is not saintly, it is dysfunctional. It is your sacred duty to safeguard the divine heritage you have received from the Infinite's hand.

81. Power and light are inseparably connected. To seek light, while with false humility shunning power, is a contradiction.

82. The correlation between energy and consciousness demands that you treat your energy as a priceless possession. To squander energy is to disrespect consciousness.

83. The essence of abundant living is found in generosity of expression, not in depleting our environment by taking more than we need.

84. Give lavishly whenever you can. The right question to ask is "What is the most I can give?", rather than "What is the most I can get for the least I can give?"

85. To fulfill your heart's desires before those of someone else allows you to give to others from a position of wholeness.

86. Feeling unlovable, many settle for feeling needed. Lovingly parent your inner child, for it is the birthplace of self-worth.

87. Being open to receiving as well as giving is to know that we are a player on the stage of life, and that in performing either role we honor the value of the play.

88. In the adventure of life we are required to perform many roles. In believing them to be real, they become identities. Identity traps awareness and hinders spiritual evolution.

89. The student seeks truth. The master creates truth spontaneously in the moment.

90. When deep elation fills your soul, you have just lived your highest truth.

91. To seek truth within already existing belief systems is to swim around and around the walls of our self-made fish bowl. Only in the silence of the mind can original thinking take place.

92. The silent mind is the seat of genius - the place of original thought where effortless knowing takes place.

93. Reason predicts the future based on the past, thereby perpetuating the past. Only the heart can guide us through the uncharted territory of moments yet to come.

94. Life's burdens consists of unyielded insights. We either die to our old way of being each day through deep, meaningful living for all of our eternal life, or we invite death to relieve us

95. The only true tragedy is a fruitless life. Failing to gain the insights of experience squanders life and invites unpleasant lessons.

96. Ingratitude stems from lack of awareness and the failure to see the multiple miracles unfolding around us. Mind demands the sensational, but the heart embraces the subtle.

97. Inspiration arises when we uncover the perfection
underlying appearances.

98. Live your life as a cause, not an effect. Respond only when and if
necessary. Fools react, masters respond.

99. Do this day the tasks allotted for it, but live as though you have
eternity. Mortality and linear time are only illusions.

100. Meditation is the finger pointing at the moon. Reach for the moon and do not over-focus on the finger. Living with complete attention and surrendering to the moment accomplishes this.

101. Do not fear adversity. What is a symphony without its low notes? When the storm winds blow through the seasons of your life, the loving embrace of the Infinite will shelter you.

102. No life is unimportant. No strand can be removed from the spiderweb of life without disturbing its perfection.

103. There is only one choice in the cosmos: what is life-enhancing.
Choose from your largest identity rather than
from your lowest limitations.

104. Forgiveness assumes guilt. True forgiveness knows there is nothing
to forgive. No one can do anything to us without our having called it in
or agreed to it.

105. Enlightenment is a journey, not a camp. There is never a point of
arrival. Let the journey therefore be a grand adventure.

106. The most virulent weed in the garden of mastery is self pity. Its twin, self-importance, is not much less noxious. Preventing them from taking root is a constant process.

107. Trust comes from knowing we are connected to Source. Courage comes from extending beyond the boundaries of our comfort zone, the place where all new knowledge is gained.

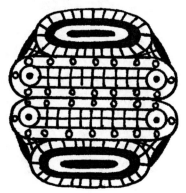

108. The heart does not open until the mind has been silenced. Only then will the infinite preciousness of life reveal itself.

109. Watch carefully the ripples of irritation in the river of your life. They are not a hindrance, but a help. Beneath the ripples lie the prevalent insights required to further your growth.

110. A life of unyielded insights is shallow, creating the internal dialogue of the mind that traps one in the world of appearances.

111. One of the greatest resources of guidance is found in the signs in our environment. Failing to heed them or to become literate in their language is tragic.

112. Many say they seek truth, but instead seek to confirm already held belief systems. Their prison bars of belief thus grow thicker and thicker.

113. The cohesive force of the cosmos is relationship. Only the most profane dare enter the temple of learning through relationship with anything other than profound reverence.

114. Noise pulls us from this moment into the next, where linear time resides. Treasure moments of silence, they allow the tension of linear time to leave your body.

115. Approaching food with the desire to gain its nutrition is to taint it with an agenda. Instead, share the abundance of its life-force by savoring it with appreciation.

116. True listening takes place in the absence of thought. Only then can you enter into the experience of another's world. To truly listen to someone else is to assimilate a new perspective.

117. Most waste energy wishing their lives would change. Masters change their environment by changing themselves.

118. A master cannot afford to indulge even the smallest blind spot in his or her vision. A grain of sand is not small in the mechanism of a watch.

119. Look for truth everywhere. Even a clock that does not work is right twice a day. The biggest fool may yet reveal the highest wisdom.

120. The most immediate way to gain power is to see what you have never seen before. Seeing further than your mind can grasp will set you free from the tyranny of surface mind.

121. The highest form of compassion is to surround yourself with those who inspire joy and to shun those who do not. Because opposite frequency attracts, your joy will automatically be attracted to the most joyless place on earth.

122. Humility is not to believe you are less than another. That merely pays homage to the other's arrogance. Humility is acknowledging that every life has equal value.

123. Character is formed one choice at a time. However, two ingredients always present are firmness with oneself and gentleness with others.

124. Discernment is born of the heart. Judgment is of the mind. The mind, unlike the heart, can only draw its conclusions from face values – this is judgment.

125. One's first duty is to preserve the sanctity of the heart and the stillness of the mind. In this way, one can then render the highest service.

126. A lower level of existence explores life by examining ways that life is *not*. A higher life explores the beauty and purity of what *is*.

127. The vast number of inner senses, consisting of pure emotions and states of being, provide a far greater wealth of guidance as to what is life-enhancing than the five outer senses.

128. Learning to love without pain and live without agenda is humanity's greatest challenge.

129. Do not try and 'fix' your shortcomings. They are not there by accident. They are the indicators of areas where life is waiting to reveal itself.

130. Create a sacred space by expressing passionately. The denser you
find your environment, the greater the need to push
the density back with your passion.

131. If you have become a stranger to passion, find its tracks within your
joy. The deeper you go into joy, the more your passion will reveal itself,
for they are partners in the joyous discovery of life.

132. If you pacify the petty tyrants of your life for the sake of keeping
peace, you will instead be promoting tyranny. In not learning the
lessons they come to impart, you keep them on their treadmill
of being unpleasant perception givers.

133. In living from your highest identity as a consciousness superimposed over all that is, the cosmos becomes your resource library. Breathe in the timelessness of the stars, the newness of the dawn, the fluid grace of the river.

134. The hollows carved in your soul by the winters of your life are the fertile hollows where seeds of joy can grow. The master never envies the one who lives a seasonless life where seeds have to grow in shallow ground.

135. Most who seek abundance, instead focus on their perceived lack, thereby strengthening it. See yourself as part of the abundance of Creation. There are trillions of field flowers, of grains of sand, of stars. Your body too consists of abundant life. Let your affirmation be: "I am abundance."

136. If you steadfastly hold before you the desires of your heart, life will present you with opportunities to fulfill them. Each day, watch carefully for unopened doors to knock on. Your heart will tell you which ones to step through when they open.

137. Fulfillment begins by rejoicing in what you have. Change begins in accepting where you are. Increase begins in being grateful for your supply.

138. Critical thinking without creative thinking is destructive. Creative thinking without critical thinking perpetuates mediocrity. The heart bypasses both through effortless knowing.

139. Disillusionment in the reliability of the external to supply our needs
is a great blessing. It gifts us with the knowledge that our being is our
sustenance.

140. What we attempt to control will produce volatility instead.
The only control we may ever have is self-control.

141. There are those who build and those who tear down.
What makes the difference is not being afraid to fail.

142. Lasting friendships must inspire mutual growth to be life-enhancing. The only other way they could be lasting is through conformity – the death knell of greatness.

143. Fly where your heart takes you, inspired and unafraid. He who waits for the approval of others has clipped his own wings.

144. Apathy is the key ingredient of mediocrity. Greatness watches for moments in which a contribution to life can be made.

BOOK THREE

The Alchemical Potencies
of Light

"The root of alchemy can be found in the
potencies of the colors of light."

Second Transmission from the Infinite

Now you must know of the 300 potencies of light: 300 there are in each of the three primary colors, red, yellow and blue. Each color has 300 nuances, or depths of color if you wish to describe it so.

The fracturing of light, although it occurred through contraction, has brought about this depth of knowledge. Conveying to My children the methods for utilizing the potencies of light would not have been possible, had light not separated and revealed its magnificence at the dawn of individuated life.

The separation of light into its three primary colors of red, which expands, yellow, which in turn holds the boundaries, and blue, which contracts, is this day changed.

Yellow's old program of keeping rigid boundaries now provides balance, stability and contentment. Memories about having to attack anything threatening the status quo need to be removed. Yellow represents the frequency of praise and must also be cleared of impurities. All memories of praise being used to manipulate, with an agenda or only for 'doing' versus 'being', must be cleared.

Red's memories that it had caused the fracturing to occur and brought about duress by asking contradictory questions, needs to be healed. Its feeling that there is a price to pay for its expansion, which causes blue to contract, must also be healed. The frequency of red is gratitude. The perception that gratitude can only be for what we receive or achieve, rather than for what we have, must be cleared.

Blue has memories of victimhood, of being plunged into the captivity of the dream state by red. Therefore it does not trust red's expansion and when red tries to do so, blue contracts. Its emotion is love, but love cannot exist in the absence of trust or in the presence of fear.

Let this be cleared this day.

Let all three colors be cleared of the memory that there is a need for aggression to defend their function.

There is instability when these three primary colors are separated. The masculine pole of yellow should be joined to the red's feminine, creating orange. The feminine pole of the yellow should be joined to the masculine part of blue, making green. The masculine pole of the red should be joined to the feminine of the blue, making purple. Then all are joined into a field that is white light. This information is necessary to properly wield the potencies of light.

The plant kingdom has the ability to turn light into chlorophyll and utilize its potency in a life-giving way. The first level of alchemy of light I shall give you uses plants as an interface.

Questions Answered by the Infinite

Q. What is the language that is being given to one of the masters? I saw it before, about a year ago.

A. It is the language of red light.

Q. Does each color have its own language?

A. Yes. Each color has 300 glyphs that create the language.

Q. How then can there be communication between the colors?

A. As of this day there is a language spoken by all colors; the language of white light.

Q. What do the 300 glyphs found in each color represent?

A. There are depths of color in each – the red, the yellow, the blue – 100 shades in each color. Each shade is bonded to a specific frequency.

Q. You mean like an emotional quality?

A. Exactly. Altogether the colors make white light. Combined, the frequencies, or tones, make the one note of creation found in incorruptible holy matter: Adoration in Action.

Q. Why did I have to redo the 300 glyphs of the red light?

A. The qualities of the red light were not inclusive enough. They created possibilities of war among My creations.

Q. You mean as here on Earth?

A. A world war, yes.

Q. When doing this alchemical magic, can one use a proxy in the circle as in the usual alchemical procedures, such as a photo or a drawing?

A. No, the circle you create is just to enclose you, the practitioner. If you are working on a person or an animal, they have to be *outside* the circle.

Q. Is there any alchemical magic that is done using these circles of the sacred wheels of the Cat People that does not use the plants as an interface between the light potencies and the physical?

A. Not at this level.

Q. Are the actual plants used or just their symbols?

A. Just their symbols.

Q. I begin to see. The symbol works with a specific *aspect* of the plant, the ability to turn light into physical results comes into play! Possibly hundreds of times more potent than the plant's obvious properties ...

A. No, thousands of times.

Q. When making the essential oils, would it enhance them to leave them in the circle of sacred wheels overnight?

A. No, when you leave the circle it must be closed down, dismantling it from the inner circles of wheels to the outer, picking them up in a counter-clockwise way.

Q. When we create the circle, we lay first the outer one in a clockwise way?

A. Yes, working your way inward, laying the center down last.

Q. How can we maximize our abilities to work with this alchemy of light?

A. By getting to know the plants involved.

The Sacred Wheels of the Cat People

The potent mysteries long guarded by the Cat People, masters of frequency and light, called the Hinig-vavaa, are being released in their pristine purity. This body of knowledge is incorruptible in its use to manifest pure intent.

Multiple layers of the mysteries can be received from them at this time. The first layer, given here, needs to be honored and respectfully received by man as the foundation for the other portions of the information. This first layer involves the use of the sacred wheels of the Cat People. There are four master wheels that work with the DNA wheels of humans, plants and animals, one master wheel serving as a portal and focal point and 24 wheels that activate light and frequencies. These 24 wheels form the boundary of the area influenced by the potencies of light.

Transmission from the Cat People

Received by Eva

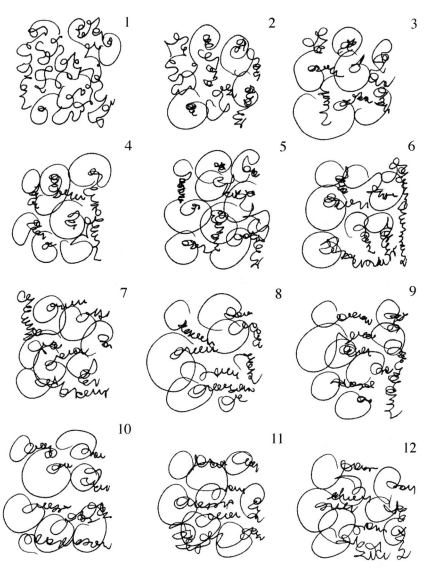

Translation of the Glyphs of the Cat People

1. *Zhanug bing haa-uvaving waa-oova banit.*
   Cleanse that which is held as sacred by us.

2. *Baanoo pivit hushaa minuwa paheem esaa zunahim.*
   Our magic holds corruption within its heart.

3. *Gaanig bee-uusaa vaa-oovahim Basta zanug.*
   The Goddess Bast seized its power for herself.

4. *Kaaneesh wahanus paasut alasta misat.*
   Abused by dark sorcerers who seek power.

5. *Kaanich haarish vasta oovaa waa nusat.*
   Some do magic to blind the eyes of men.

6. *Kaash oosat hashet manusat savi.*
   They seem as leaders of wisdom to some.

7. *Kaanush habasat paashut zaa ninit.*
   Originally these sacred powers were pure.

8. *Traa his waanusavaa kanavik pilsat.*
   They could only be used for good.

9. *Koonis bistoo ars haras pahur.*
   Take away from imposters their ability to misuse.

10. *Ku-oohasta minuwa oosit archstava.*
    Let their barrenness of virtue be shown.

11. *Pineesh heste ish Hinig-vavaa.*
    We are the Hinig-vavaa.

12. *Zhong-Galabruk ekle birit alestaa stu-avach.*
    We are related to, but different from the Zhong-Galabruk

Third Transmission from the Infinite

I tell now the general qualities of the stable combinations of light. For in wielding the alchemical potencies inherent in light, the colors must never be used separately, but only in combination.

1. The First 100 Equations

In the first 100 equations the positive, pro-active aspect of the blue light and the negative, receptive aspect of the yellow light are the most dominant – green. The dominant characteristic quality is *creative*. It is to be used to create what was not there before, such as abundance, fertility, solutions and so forth. Creation can only occur in alignment with My intent and will not respond to anything else. The alchemy of light is incorruptible.

2. The Second 100 Equations

The second 100 equations have red and yellow as the most dominant colors. The negative, or receptive aspect of red and the positive, pro-active aspect of yellow determine the predominant characteristic of expansion – expressed in the color orange. These 100 equations enhance, expand and augment that which already exists. They would be used for growth in any area of life. The red/yellow dominance helps create dynamic balance to prevent stagnation. The blue/yellow combination prevents instability, especially where growth is rapid. They also produce contentment.

3. **The Third 100 Equations**

The third 100 equations, using red and blue to make purple, have predominantly cleansing qualities. The positive, pro-active aspect of red and the feminine, receptive aspect of blue are accentuated for the purposes of purification, cleansing and the restoration of purity and innocence. This color combination is the only one that cannot be used to assist with balance.

Miracle Story

(by the oracle Shelley in Toronto, Canada)

On January 5, 2009, at approximately 2:00 am, Almine suddenly appeared in my home in Toronto and gave me the following information:

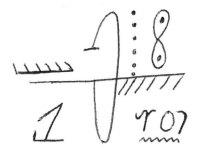

Meeshka ala oesta maj eta
New programs for balancing light
and frequency

"Change the direction from within to without
Once again man shall flourish"

Explanation:

For life to flourish, the new functions given to light are opposite to what they were before. That which expands is the positive aspect of blue light and the negative aspect of yellow light. Previously the blue contracted and the yellow held constricting boundaries.

The Placement of the Wheels of the Cat People

24 small wheels
around the edge
placed in a circle

North

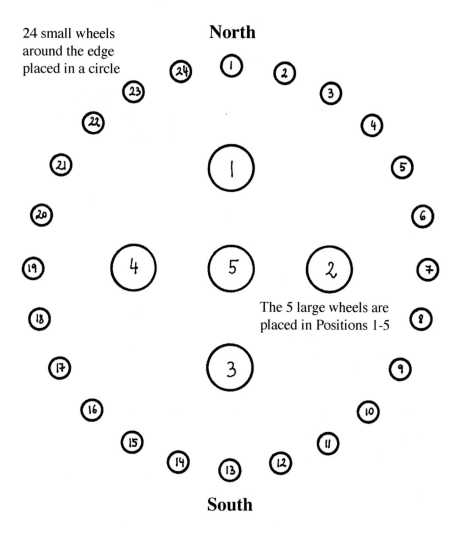

The 5 large wheels are
placed in Positions 1-5

South

The DNA wheels are placed under wheels 1, 2, 3 and 4. The plant is
placed on wheel 5. You will be positioned between the ring of 5 large
wheels of Cat Magic and the ring of 24 small wheels of Cat Magic.

Drawn by Eva

What You Will Need to Use for the Alchemical Potencies of Light

1. Deciding What You Want to Work On

Identify your target of influence. Is it a location where there are just humans, such as an office or school? Is it a place where animals will be affected, such as a home with pets? Perhaps you are working on an orchard or wheat field in which case the effects will be on plants only. Based on what you have determined, you will require:

    4 Wheels of Human DNA
       and/or
    4 Wheels of Animal DNA
       and/or
    4 Wheels of Plant DNA

2. Creating a Circle of 24 Small Wheels of Cat Magic

From the 24 small wheels, you will need to create a circle around you (starting with Wheel 1 in the North), laying them down in a clockwise manner.

3. Creating a Circle of 5 Large Wheels of Cat Magic

You will need the 5 large wheels of Cat Magic. Place Wheel 1 in the North as shown in "The Placement of the Wheels of the Cat People" on page 97, Wheel 2 in the East, Wheel 3 in the South, Wheel 4 in the West and Wheel 5 in the Center.

4. Choosing the DNA Wheels

Based on which of the DNA Wheels you will be using, place them *under* the large wheels of the Cat People as follows:

(a)   If more than one set of DNA wheels are used, put the *human DNA*

on top, then the *animal DNA below* that and the *plant DNA* at the
bottom.

Remember: **HUMAN DNA WHEELS MUST ALWAYS BE ON TOP**
of any other DNA wheels used.

(b) Any No. 1 DNA wheels are stacked beneath the large No. 1 wheel of
the Cat People (remember, large wheel No. 5 is in the middle – there are
no DNA wheels stacked beneath No. 5).

No. 2 DNA wheels are stacked beneath the large wheel No. 2. No. 3
DNA wheels are stacked beneath the large wheel No. 3; No. 4 DNA
wheels are stacked beneath the large wheel No. 4.

5. Choosing the Best Alchemical Equation

Carefully study the 300 alchemical equations to determine which one to
use.

Only one equation is used at a time. If you determine that a
cleansing equation is needed before an enhancing one, the procedure is
repeated. When completed with the first equation, while remaining in
your circle, replace it with the second equation and repeat the process.
Note: When an equation is replaced with one using a different plant as
an interface – see **6. Choosing the Correct Plant Symbol** on the next
page – that will have to be replaced as well.

Place your equation on top of the large No. 5 wheel of Cat People in
the middle of the circle.

Remember, in studying the equations to determine which are best
suited for your purpose, they fall into three categories:

Equations 1-100 – creating that which was not there before and
producing stability.

Equations 101-200 – enhancing that which already exists and preventing
stagnation.

Equations 201-300 – cleansing and restoring purity and equity as well as removing illusion.

6. Choosing the Correct Plant Symbol

There are 12 plant symbols used as interfaces with light. Each plant is used for 25 of the equations. Based on a specific equation chosen by you, the related plant symbol needs to be identified and used. The plant symbol is place on top of the equation on the center-most wheel.

The Twelve Plants and their Equations

1. Cumin	Equations 1-25
2. Fern	Equations 26-50
3. Cedar	Equations 51-75
4. Cucumber	Equations 76-100
5. Nasturtium	Equations 101-125
6. Lupine	Equations 126-150
7. Strawberry	Equations 151-175
8. Rye	Equations 176-200
9. Sweet Pea	Equations 201-225
10. Mustard	Equations 226-250
11. Yam	Equations 251-275
12. Jicama	Equations 276-300

7. Reading out the Names of the 24 Small Wheels of Cat Magic

You will need a list of the names of the 24 small wheels to read out during the alchemical activation. After reading them, you will speak the words of activation. Proceed as follows:

"I activate the 24 Wheels of Alchemical Potencies by calling their names."

1. Nitva

2. Burna

3. Sabatu

4. Hirmanut

5. Evanut

6. Wasabil

7. Usanu
8. Kilirut
9. Silmani
10. Britvuba
11. Ellesut
12. Kaleshvu
13. Nichtu
14. Plubavi
15. Hellestut

16. Arikdoch
17. Burtlnut
18. Vaaruk
19. Kirtldom
20. Arechva
21. Nuselvavi
22. Garanut
23. Eleshklavi
24. Baarom

8. Speaking the Words of Alchemical Activation
"Let the language of light be activated.
Let the equations' power be sent to:
(specify where the influence is to be directed)"

Ninach haresva ukleshbi naruset.
Viskel arat parenu asklavaa.
Vilesach bifit arenuesva halesbi.
Tri-unar este barunish.

You have now completed your work with the alchemical potencies of light. You may either remove the equation and plant symbol, replacing it with another equation and plant symbol, and repeat the words over again, or close your circles down as previously described on page 91.

The Language of the Holy Mother

(Excerpted from *The Ring of Truth*)

Pronunciation of Mother's Language
  The pronunciation is very much like German, other than that the 'v' (as in very) and 'w' (as in white) are pronounced as in English.

The syllables are pronounced individually when placed next to each other. There are no contracted sounds like 'au' (as in trauma). It would be necessary to say the 'a' and 'u' separately. The only exception to this rule is a double 'aa' at the end of a word. This indicates the 'a' sound (as in spa). The 'ch' spelling at the beginning of a word is the only time it is pronounced as in 'church'. Everywhere else it is pronounced as in the German 'kirche' or somewhat like the Spanish x as in Mexico.

- 'u' is pronounced as in 'prudence'.
- 'a' is pronounced as in 'garden'.
- 'e' is as in 'pet'.
- 'i' is pronounced as in 'pink'.
- 'o' is pronounced in the way someone with an English accent would say 'of' or 'cross'.
- 'g' is always a hard 'g' like 'great'.
- 'c' is always hard as in 'call'.
- 'q' has a 'qw' sound as in 'queen'.
- 'r' is slightly rolled—'rr'.
- 'y' is pronounced as in 'Yvette', with an 'ee' sound.

There are many words for 'I' or 'is' because of frequency changes. "I am happy" has a much higher frequency than "I am tired", and "I" or "am" would therefore be different in each of these sentences.

Also, when the concept is large, several words are needed. 'Beautiful' will have different words depending on what is described, but in each case the term will have several words since it is a complex concept.

There are no words for 'sad', 'pain', 'angry', 'protective' or 'fear', since those are illusory concepts in this creation of life. There are also no negative words.

'I' and 'we' would be the same word as this is a group consciousness language. Similarly, 'he' and 'they' would use the same word.

Sentences and Phrases:

1. *Aushbava heresh sishisim* (Come here)
2. *Va-aal vi-ish paru-es* (Do it again)

3. *Kre-eshna sa-ul varavaa* (It is beautiful everywhere)
4. *Pranuvaa sanuvesh vilsh-savu bravispa* (We are with you when you think of us)
5. *Aasushava pre-unan aruva bareesh* (We come to open the gate)
Note: 'Come' in this sense is not the same word used for 'come here'.
6. *Oonee varunish heshpiu tra barin* (Everyone is dancing with joy)
7. *Belesh bri anur bra vershpi iulan* (Take away the frown from your face)
8. *Nen hursh avervi tranuk averva?* (When comes the moment of laughing?) Note: there is no word for time.
9. *Nun brash barnut pareshvi* (Please take us with you)
10. *Vursh venestu parneshtu* (Magic is in the moment)
11. *Iuvishpa niutrim sarem* (Great things await)
12. *Ruftravasbi iulem* (Let the fun begin)
13. *Verluash verurlabaa mi urla set viunish* (Be prepared for the fulfillment of your dreams)
14. *Be-ulahesh parve mi-ur ville starva* (Speak to us through these sacred words)
15. *Truaveshviesh aluvispaha maurnanuhe* (Welcome to the fullness of our being)
16. *Telech nusva rura vesbi* (Through love are we connected)
17. *Erluech spauhura vavish menuba* (Find the new song that you sing)
18. *Me-uhu vaubaresh ka-ur-tum* (Our new dance is a joyous one)
19. *Pelech parve uru-uhush vaspa pe-uravesh ple-ura* (Together let us create wonderous moments)
20. *Vala veshpa uvi kle-u vishpi ula usbeuf pra-uva* (You are invited into the loving embrace of our arms)
21. *Perenuesh krava susibreve truach* (In great mercy you are renewed)
22. *Pleshpaa vu skaura versebia nunuhesh* (Allow your shoulders to feel lightness)
23. *Verunachva ulusetvaabi manuresh* (All are in this moment redeemed)
24. *Keleustraha virsabaluf bra uvraha* (You dwell in us and are ours)
25. *Keleshpruanesh te le-usbaru* (Call and we shall hear)

Alphabet of The Holy Mother

1. AUX

2. PAH

3. GHEE

4. KA

5. G as in Gold

6. DJU as in Giraffe

7. B

8. PE as in Peg

9. L

10. TRA

11. I as in Ink

12. N

13. R

14. A as in Far

15. M

16. E as in Leg

17. U as in True

18. V

19. SH

20. K

21. H

22. S

23. O as in Open

24. Y as in Yvette ("ee" sound)

25. QW as in Quai

26. T

27. CH as in Church

28. A as in Back

29. O as in Lock

30. XCH as in Mexico (Spanish pronunciation)

31. F

32. Z as in Azure (soft sound)

33. RR (rolled r)

34. P

35. Y as in Yes

36. CK (short K sound)

37. Period (placed at the end of a sentence)

38. Question mark (placed at the beginning of a sentence)

1. D

2. PF

3. KL

4. W

5. SHP

6. KRR

7. HF

8. PL

9. TL

The Language of the Holy Mother

Magic is in the
moment.
(vursh venes-
tu parneshtu)

Great things
await.
(luvishpa
niutrim sarem)

Let the fun
begin.
(Ruftra-
vasbi iulem)

Please take me with
you. (Nun brash bar-
nut pareshvi)

Plant Symbol #1: Cumin

Plant Symbol #2: Fern

Plant Symbol #3: Cedar

Plant Symbol #4: Cucumber

Plant Symbol #5: Nasturtium

Plant Symbol #6: Lupine

Plant Symbol #7: Strawberry

Plant Symbol #8: Rye

Plant Symbol #9: Sweet Pea

Plant Symbol #10: Mustard

Plant Symbol #11: Yam

Plant Symbol #12: Jicama

Wheel of Human DNA #1

Wheel of Human DNA #2

Wheel of Human DNA #3

Wheel of Human DNA #4

Wheel of Animal DNA #1

Wheel of Animal DNA #2

Wheel of Animal DNA #3

Wheel of Animal DNA #4

Wheel of Plant DNA #1

Wheel of Plant DNA #2

Wheel of Plant DNA #3

Wheel of Plant DNA #4

Large Wheel #1 - Cat People Magic

Large Wheel #2 - Cat People Magic

Large Wheel #3 - Cat People Magic

Large Wheel #4 - Cat People Magic

Large Wheel #5 - Cat People Magic

Nitva, Small Wheel #1 - Cat People Magic

Burna, Small Wheel #2 - Cat People Magic

Sabatu, Small Wheel #3 - Cat People Magic

Hirmanut, Small Wheel #4 - Cat People Magic

Evanut, Small Wheel #5 - Cat People Magic

Wasabil, Small Wheel #6 - Cat People Magic

Usanu, Small Wheel #7 - Cat People Magic

Kilirut, Small Wheel #8 - Cat People Magic

Silmani, Small Wheel #9 - Cat People Magic

Britvuba, Small Wheel #10 - Cat People Magic

Ellesut, Small Wheel #11 - Cat People Magic

Kaleshvu, Small Wheel #12 - Cat People Magic

Nichtu, Small Wheel #13 - Cat People Magic

Plubavi, Small Wheel #14 - Cat People Magic

Hellestut, Small Wheel #15 - Cat People Magic

Arikdoch, Small Wheel #16 - Cat People Magic

Burtlnut, Small Wheel #17 - Cat People Magic

Vaaruk, Small Wheel #18 - Cat People Magic

Kirtldom, Small Wheel #19 - Cat People Magic

Arechva, Small Wheel #20 - Cat People Magic

Nuselvavi, Small Wheel #21 - Cat People Magic

Garanut, Small Wheel #22 - Cat People Magic

Eleshklavi, Small Wheel #23 - Cat People Magic

Baarom, Small Wheel #24 - Cat People Magic

(1) Abundant Supply

(2) Bountiful Increase

(3) Flourishing Endeavors

(4) Unlimited Success

149

(5) Increasing Accomplishments

(6) Beneficial Results

(7) Unexpected Bounty

(8) Created Affluence

151

(9) Hopeful Aspirations

(10) Realized Dreams

(11) Fruitful Labor

(12) Life's Bounteous Gifts

(13) Exceeded Expectations

(14) Recognizing Opportunities

(15) Daring to Excel

(16) Excellence Achieved

(17) Believing in Self-achievement

(18) Grand Expectation

(19) Seizing the Moment

(20) Unforeseen Possibilities

(21) Recognizing Life's Bounty

(22) The Joy of the Flight

(23) The Conquering of Self

(24) Measured Expansion

(25) Created New Paradigms

(26) Untold Possibilities

(27) Fertile Exploration

(28) Uncovering Life's Bounty

(29) Exploring Inner Horizons

(30) Limitless Capabilities

(31) Imaginative Solutions

(32) Enthusiastic Participation in Life

(33) Growth Through Divine Alignment

(34) Following Inner Promptings

(35) Defying All Limitation

(36) Individual Excellence

(37) Graceful Expansion

(38) Unlimited Attainment

(39) Claiming Divine Inheritance

(40) Light-Hearted Achievement

(41) Igniting Passion

(42) Trying the New

(43) Finding Innovative Pathways

(44) Spontaneous Creation of Truth

(45) Supported Expansion

(46) Faith-Based Optimism

(47) Becoming All-Abundant

(48) Fluid Flowering of Life

(49) Seeing Discerned Options

(50) Life-Enhancing Acquisitions

(51) Limitless Possibilities

(52) Cooperating Flight

(53) Embracing the Wind

(54) Expecting Perfection

(55) Enchanting Journey

(56) Delightful Encounters

(57) Confidence Born of Self-Belief

(58) Energetic Exploration

(59) Unknown Discoveries

(60) Inspiring Imagination

(61) Confident Strategies

(62) Heartfelt Guidance

(63) Complete Fluidity

(64) Unencumbered Journey

(65) Enjoyment of the Adventure

(66) Exuberant Self-Expression

(67) Articulated Desires

(68) Unsurpassed Beauty Discovered

(69) Answering the Call of Divine Intent

(70) Creative Zeal

(71) Acknowledged Perfection

(72) Inspired Vision

183

(73) Enthusiastic Implementation

(74) Self-Motivating Perception

(75) Visionary Incentive

(76) Entrusted Mission

(77) Unconditional Oneness & Cooperation

(78) Joy-Promoting Accomplishments

(79) Steady Progress

(80) Supported Exponential Growth

(81) Provided Blessings for Conviction

(82) Sustenance for the Journey

(83) Garnering Needed Resources

(84) Extending Our Reach

189

(85) Freedom of Flight

(86) Acknowledging Oneness

(87) Full Surrender to the Currents of Life

(88) Humble Approach to the Unknown

(89) Impeccable Consideration of Consequences

(90) Accomplishments Benefitting All

(91) Freedom Through Self-Responsibility

(92) Grateful Acknowledgement of Progress

(93) Effortless Harvest of Gifts

(94) Mastery in Action

(95) Responding to Spontaneity

(96) Promoting Pristine Creativity

(97) Valuing the Quality of the Journey

(98) Honoring Contributions of Others

196

(99) Agenda-Less Aspirations

(100) Fully Cooperative Living

(101) Fluid Structure

(102) Contented Foundations

(103) Unconditional Support

(104) Blissful Expansions

(105) All-Inclusive Presence

(106) Complete Self-Responsibility

(107) Dynamic Balance

(108) Holding Multiple Perspectives

(109) Maintaining the Reference Point

(110) Grounding Flight

(111) Augmented Wellbeing

(112) Creating a Stable Inner Home

(113) Sheltered Innocence

(114) Valuing Beingness

(115) Non-Directional Expansion of Light

(116) All-Encompassing Peace

(117) Trusting Divine Synchronicities

(118) Inclusive Compassion

(119) Expanded Awareness

(120) Unshakeable Serenity

(121) Ever-Present Poise

(122) Graceful Interaction

(123) Interactive Dance

(124) Supportive Strength

(125) Embracing Warmth

(126) Firm Foundation

(127) Vistas of Distant Horizons

(128) Culminating Bliss

(129) Ecstatic Embrace

(130) Delightful Companionship

(131) Depth of Praise

(132) Height of Gratitude

213

(133) Cherishing Presence

(134) Comforting Stability

(135) Expanding Inclusiveness

(136) Bridging Viewpoints

(137) Consoling Comforter

(138) Deepening Understanding

(139) Expanding Abilities

(140) All-Knowing Silence

(141) Guiding Light

(142) Increased Supply

(143) Endless Resources

(144) Hope Embodied

(145) Original Knowing

(146) Effortless Accomplishment

(147) Honoring Diversity

(148) Supporting Growth

(149) Supply of Power

(150) Accommodating Fluidity

(151) Entrusted Care

(152) Holistic Accomplishment

(153) Balancing Individual Expression

(154) Orderly Flexibility

(155) Inner Nurturing

(156) Spiritual Succor

(157) Engendering Fullness of Living

(158) Creating an Arena of Expression

(159) Upholding Heartfelt Desires

(160) Creative Muse

(161) Ancient Embrace

(162) Sacred Stewardship

(163) Inseparable Union

(164) Eternal Fluid Moment

(165) Effortless Transfigurative Regeneration

(166) Seeing the Perfection

(167) Stirred by the Song of Life

(168) Adoration of the One Life

(169) Aligned with Infinite Intent

(170) Cooperative Endeavor

(171) Boundless Increase

(172) Silent Mind

233

(173) Full Surrender

(174) Wonderment at the Glory

(175) Complete Trust in the Infinite

(176) Un-imagined Vistas

(177) Stirring Inspiration

(178) Herald of Hopeful Anticipation

(179) Purity Expressed

(180) Enlightenment

237

(181) Fulfilled Feeling

(182) Steadfast Equanimity

238

(183) Timeless Rest

(184) Deep Appreciation

(185) Permeating Contentment

(186) Unflappable Mastery

(187) Deep Homage to Life

(188) Innocent Enjoyment

(189) Refined Expression

(190) Elegant Fluid Patterns

(191) Transient Permanence

(192) Graceful Transition

(193) Implementing Expectations of Peace

(194) Living in Abundance

(195) Self-Dignity Restored

(196) Balance Distribution of Resources

(197) Fully Available Wealth of Sacred Treasures

(198) Loving Gratitude for Life

(199) Resounding Praise for Diverse Contributions

(200) Acknowledged Perfection of Divine Intent

(201) Dissolving All Limitations

(202) Ruthless Self-honesty

(203) Relinquishing Control

(204) Erasing Programs of Strife

(205) Effortlessly Dissolving the Obsolete
by Expansion of Consciousness

(206) Eliminating the Obsolete

(207) Replacing Mediocrity with Excellence

(208) Unconditional Compliance with Divine Intent

(209) Eradicating Self-Centeredness

(210) Replacing Divisiveness with Inclusiveness

(211) Exposing Intrinsic Value

(212) Purification of Discordance

(213) Exposing what is Real

(214) Removing All Sub-creations of Man

(215) Acknowledging Bounty

(216) Feeling Connected to Source

(217) Seeing Perfection Behind Appearances

(218) Believing in Beneficial Life

(219) Self-Determined Success

(220) Authentic Living

(221) Absolute Truth

(222) Triumphant Expression of Inner Divinity

(223) Agenda-Less Generosity

(224) Unencumbered Journey

(225) Self-Referring Approval

(226) Justice Triumphant

(227) Unseen Motives Exposed

(228) Innocence Victorious

(229) The Flourishing of the Worthy

(230) Unimpeccability Demolished

(231) Righteous Leadership

(232) Honoring Stewardship

(233) Ensnarements Disentangled

(234) Predators Eliminated

(235) Conspirators Confounded

(236) Promoters of Confusion Dissolved

(237) Respecting the Planet

(238) Preserving the Environment

(239) Memories of Injury Healed

(240) Arrogance Brought Low

(241) Corruption Removed

(242) Purity Preserved

(243) Obsolete History Forgotten

(244) Injurious Strategies Undone

(245) Magnificent Mastery

(246) Self-Disciplined Clarity

(247) Death Defeated

(248) Immortality Embraced

(249) Achievements Beyond Mortal Boundaries

(250) Exposing Injustice through Acquiescence

(251) Removal of Incompetent Stewardship

(252) Opening Hearts to Compassion

273

(253) Breaking the Tyranny of Social Conditioning

(254) Freeing the Mind of Man

(255) Opening the Inner Senses

(256) Unlocking All Potential

(257) Removing Programmed Unbelief

(258) Forgiving Innocent Offenses

(259) Determining True Motives

(260) Disempowering the Unethical

(261) Abolishing All Cruelty

(262) Reestablishing Respect for Animals

(263) Engendering the Cherishing of Nature

(264) Removing the Existence of Spite and Hate

(265) Cleansing All Jealousy and Envy

(266) Acknowledging the Interconnectedness of Life

(267) Dissolving Elitism

(268) Establishing the Equality of All Life

(269) Removing Obstruction to Beneficial Outcomes

(270) Recompensing the Worthy

(271) Sensitive Awareness

(272) Removing Tyranny Through Weakness

(273) Removing Obstructions to Individual Sovereignty

(274) Sacred Societies

(275) Valuing Simplicity

(276) Cutting the Ties that Bind

(277) Eliminating All Addictions

(278) Being Home for Oneself

(279) Self-Love in Action

(280) Adoration of the Infinite

(281) Song of Joy

(282) Heartsong Express Through Labor

(283) Walking a Path With Heart

(284) Abiding in the Presence of the Infinite

(285) Lightness of Being

(286) Trusting Our Feelings

(287) Bounteous Living

(288) Embracing Fluid Change

(289) Effortless Purification

(290) Honoring the Body's Holy Incorruptible Matter

(291) Deep, Meaningful Living

(292) Harmonious Interaction with the Flow of Life

(293) Joyous Expression of Individuality

(294) Revering the Diversity of Expression

(295) Compassionate Understanding

(296) Holy Covenant

(297) Indivisible Union of Light

(298) The Purified Frequencies of the Cosmic Song

(299) Living in the Infinite White Light

(300) Holy Marriage of Light and Frequency

The Placement of Wheels Used for Preparing Essential Oils

North

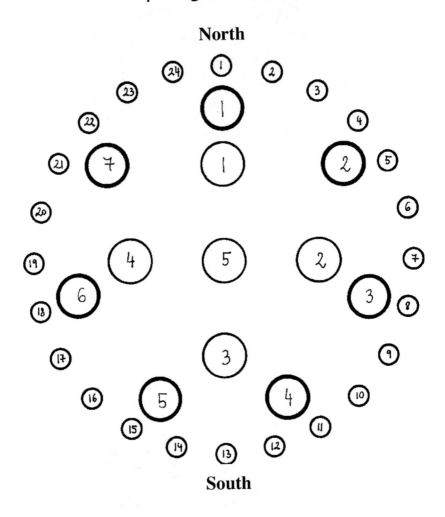

South

<u>Note:</u> This drawing is not to scale. You will be positioned between the ring of 7 wheels of the Tones of the One Note and the ring of 24 small wheels of Cat Magic.

Preparing Essential Oils

The entire alchemical process is exactly the same as described before, except the 7 wheels of the Tones of the One Note are placed as shown on the previous page. They form a circle to the inside of the 24 small wheels of Cat Magic.

As you conduct the activation, position yourself on the outside of the ring of 7 wheels of the Tones of the One Note and inside the ring of the 24 small wheels of Cat Magic. In other words, you will be between the circle of 7 wheels of the Tones of the One Note and the circle of 24 small wheels of Cat Magic.

Place a clean container (preferably glass) with food grade Almond oil – the purest oil – on top of the plant symbol in the middle. Remember, the plant symbol is on top of the equation you have chosen to place in your oil. The equation is on top of the No. 5 large wheel.

When you speak the words (the same as previously given), direct the equation's power into the oil that has been placed to receive it.

Use only wheels of human DNA for humans or wheels of animal DNA for pets.

Tone of the One Note #1: Wheel of Gratitude

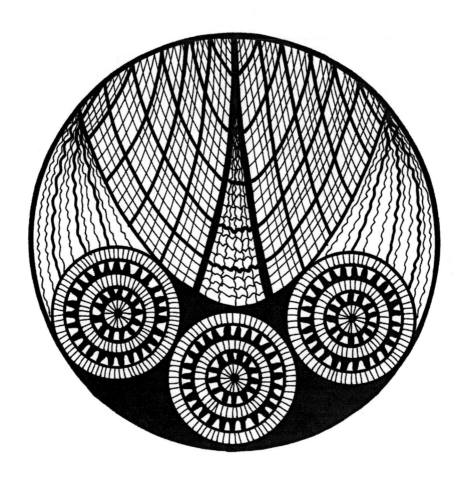

Tone of the One Note #2: Wheel of Love

Tone of the One Note #3: Wheel of Praise

Tone of the One Note #4: Wheel of Poise

Tone of the One Note #5: Wheel of Reverence

Tone of the One Note #6: Wheel of Grace

Tone of the One Note #7: Wheel of Timing

Notes on Preparing Essential Oils

1. The oil prepared is <u>for external use only</u>.

2. Even though their symbols are used, the plants themselves are never used in this alchemical process. The exception is the pure, food grade almond oil.

3. Almond oil is the only oil that can be used to prepare these alchemical oils because of the alchemical equation of the twelve plants + almond oil.

The twelve interface plants + Almond oil   = Pristine creations

Powerful infusion of light   + The womb of love = Pristine creations

(the language of alchemy)

4. *To use the oil*: Placing it on any acupuncture point is effective. The wrists, ears, feet or spine are good areas. Seven drops is the maximum dosage required.

5. <u>Never use animal oil for humans</u> (where only animal DNA wheels were used in preparation). In the case of preparing these oils, <u>do not double up the DNA wheels</u> during preparation. Either prepare it for humans or prepare an entirely different batch for animals.

6. These oils can be used in conjunction with Belvaspata, Kriyavaspata and the other mystical and healing modalities listed on the following websites:

Almine Healing
www.alminehealing.com

Ancient Shamanism
www.ancientshamanism.com

Animal Healing
www.spiritual-healing-for-animals.com

Arubafirina
www.arubafirina.com

Ascended Mastery
www.ascendedmastery.com

Ascension Angels
www.ascensionangels.com

Astrology of Isis
www.astrology-of-isis.com

Belvaspata
www.belvaspata.org

Divine Architect
www.divinearchitect.com

Earth Wisdom Chronicles
www.earthwisdomchronicles.com

Incorruptible White Magic
www.incorruptiblewhitemagic.com

Mystical Kingdoms
www.mysticalkingdoms.com

School of Arcana
www.schoolofarcana.org

Way of the Toltec Nagual
www.wayofthetoltecnagual.com

Wheels of the Goddess
www.wheelsofthegoddess.com

Closing

Since being called by the Infinite in February 2005 to assist in restoring the sacred bodies of information, my journey has been a deeply mystical one. I have been impressed with how little we have truly understood the diversity of life that surrounds us. That even a little flower growing by the wayside can hold such power and magic within its heart, has been forgotten for eons of time. It is with the deepest love for the many kingdoms around us, both seen and unseen, that I dedicate this book to the One Life expressing as the many.

Almine

Other books by Almine

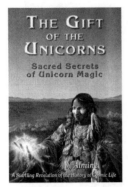

The Gift of the Unicorns *Second Edition*
Sacred Secrets of Unicorn Magic

These life-changing insights into the deep mystical secrets of the earth's past puts the cosmic role of humanity into perspective. It gives meaning to the suffering of the ages and solutions of hope and predicts the restoration of white magic. An enlightening explanation of the causes of the Great Fall and our ascent out of ages of forgetfulness into a remembrance of our divine new purpose and oneness, is masterfully given. Truly an inspiring book!

Published: 2009, 284 pages, soft cover, 6 x 9, ISBN: 978-1-934070-29-1

Opening the Doors of Heaven *Second Edition*
Revelations of the Mysteries of Isis

Through a time-travel tunnel, linking Ireland and Egypt, Isis sent a small group of masters to prepare for the day when her mysteries would once again be released to the world to restore balance and enhance life.

They established the Order of the White Rose to guard the sacred objects and the secrets of Isis. In an unprecedented event heralding the advent of a time of light, these mysteries are released for the first time.

Published: 2009, 312 pages, soft cover, 6 x 9 ISBN: 978-1-934070-31-4

Windows Into Eternity *Second Edition*
Revelations of the Mother Goddess

This book provides unparalled insight into ancient mysteries. Almine, an internationally recognized mystic and teacher, reveals the hidden laws of existence. Transcending reason, delivering visionary expansion, this metaphysical masterpiece explores the origins of life as recorded in the Holy Libraries.

The release of information from these ancient libraries is a priceless gift to humankind. The illusions found in the building blocks of existence are exposed, as are the purposes of Creation.

Published: 2009, 320 pages, soft cover, 6 x 9, ISBN: 978-1-934070-32-1

The Way of the Toltec Nagual

New Precepts for the Spiritual Warrior

Not only is this wisdom packed book a guide for serious students of the Toltec way, but also a font of knowledge for all truth-seekers. Mapping out the revolutionary changes in Toltec mysticism, it presents the precepts of mastery sought out by all who travel the road of illumination and spiritual warriorship. Almine reveals publicly for the first time, the ancient power symbols used by Toltec Naguals to assist in obtaining freedom from illusion. Bonus section: Learn about the hidden planets used by Toltecs and the Astrology of Isis.

Published: 2009, 240 pages, soft cover, 6 x 9, ISBN: 978-1-934070-56-7

CDs by Almine

Each powerful presentation has a unique musical background unaltered as channeled from Source. Truly a work of art.

The Power of Silence

Few teaching methods empty the mind, but rather fill it with more information. As one who has achieved this state of silence, Almine meticulously maps out the path that leads to this state of expanded awareness.

The Power of Self-Reliance

Cultivating self-reliance is explained as resulting from balancing the sub-personalities—key components to emotional autonomy.

Mystical Keys to Ascended Mastery

The way to overcome and transcend mortal boundaries is clearly mapped out for the sincere truth seeker.

The Power of Forgiveness

Digressing from traditional views that forgives a perceived injury, this explains the innocence of all experience. Instead of showing how to forgive a wrong, it acknowledges wholeness.

Visit Almine's website **www.spiritualjourneys.com** for workshop locations and dates, take an online workshop, listen to an internet radio show, or watch a video. Order one of Almine's many books, CD's, or an instant download.

Phone Number: 1-877-552-5646

CPSIA information can be obtained at www.ICGtesting.com
Printed in the USA
LVOW031818261211

261030LV00006B/198/P